בס"ד

לה׳ הארץ ומלואה

This Book Belongs to:

_____

Please read it to me!

Goodnight
My Friend Aleph

A Story for Little Children

Written & Illustrated by
Tova Mordechai

Hachai
PUBLISHING

Dedicated to our beloved children

Rivkah Malca, Daniella Esther and Meir

Pamela and George Rohr

Goodnight My Friend Aleph

Dedicated to my dear friend Eva Freund. T.M.

First Edition - Sivan 5749 / June 1989
Second Impression - Elul 5762 / August 2002

ISBN: 0-922613-12-5
LCCN: 94-109938

HACHAI PUBLISHING
Brooklyn, New York
Tel: 718-633-0100 - Fax: 718-633-0103
www.hachai.com - info@hachai.com

Printed in China

Glossary

B'sammim: Spices
Challah: Shabbos loaves
D'vash: Honey
Esrog: Citron fruit used on the holiday of Succos
Geshem: Rain
Havdalah: Shabbos conclusion service
Kiddush Cup: Cup used for the blessing over wine recited on Shabbos and festivals
Kippah: Yarmulke, skullcap
Lulav: Palm branch for Succos
Mezuzah: Parchment scroll inscribed with the hand-written text of 'Shema' and affixed to the doorposts of Jewish homes and buildings

Netillas Yadayim Cup: Cup for ritual washing of hands
Oaf: Chicken
Peros: Fruit
Ruach: Wind
Shofar: Ram's horn
Siddur: Prayer book
Tallis Katan: Four-cornered tasseled garment
Torah: Jewish Scripture and Oral Tradition; Five Books of Moses
Tzeddaka: Charity
Vradim: Roses
Yayin: Wine
Zeissim: Olives

Goodnight my friend Aleph,
Goodnight Eliezer Avraham Esrog,
Goodnight my friend Aleph.

Goodnight my friend Bais,
Goodnight Binyamin Baruch B'sammim,
Goodnight my friend Bais.

Goodnight my friend Gimmel,
Goodnight Gershom Geshem,
Goodnight my friend Gimmel.

Goodnight my friend Dalet,
Goodnight Dina Devora D'vash,
Goodnight my friend Dalet.

Goodnight my friend Hey,
Goodnight Hillel Havdalah Candle,
Goodnight my friend Hey.

Goodnight my friend Vav,
Goodnight Varda and Vardit Vradim,
Goodnight my friend Vav.

Goodnight my friend Zayin,
Goodnight Zerach and Zerubbavel Zeissim,
and all the Zeissim family,
Goodnight my friend Zayin.

Goodnight my friend Ches,
Goodnight Chaya Chanie Challah,
Goodnight my friend Ches.

Goodnight my friend Tes,
Goodnight Tuvya Tallis Katan,
Goodnight my friend Tes.

Goodnight my friend Yud,
Goodnight Yonasan Yerachmiel Yayin,
Goodnight my friend Yud.

Goodnight my friend Kaf,
Goodnight Kalev Kippah,
Goodnight my friend Kaf.

Goodnight my friend Lamed,
Goodnight Levi Lulav,
Goodnight my friend Lamed.

Goodnight my friend Mem,
Goodnight Moshe Menachem Mezuzah,
Goodnight my friend Mem.

Goodnight my friend Nun,
Goodnight Nassan Netillas Yadayim Cup,
Goodnight my friend Nun.

Goodnight my friend Samech,
Goodnight Sisri Sodi Siddur,
Goodnight my friend Samech.

Goodnight my friend Ayin,
Goodnight Ofra Oaf Family,
Goodnight my friend Ayin.

Goodnight my friend Pey,
Goodnight Peretz Peiros Family,
Goodnight my friend Pey.

Goodnight my friend Tzaddi,
Goodnight Tzippora Tzeddakah Box,
Goodnight my friend Tzaddi.

Goodnight my friend Koof,
Goodnight Kehas Kiddush Cup,
Goodnight my friend Koof.

Goodnight my friend Reish,
Goodnight Reuven Rafael Ruach,
Goodnight my friend Reish.

Goodnight my friend Shin,
Goodnight Shmuel Shofar,
Goodnight my friend Shin.

Goodnight my friend Tav,
Goodnight Tanchum Torah,
Goodnight my friend Tav . . .

. . . and now let's say "Shema" . . .

out loud שְׁמַע יִשְׂרָאֵל ה׳ אֱלֹקֵינוּ ה׳ אֶחָד:

whisper בָּרוּךְ שֵׁם כְּבוֹד מַלְכוּתוֹ לְעוֹלָם וָעֶד:

out loud וְאָהַבְתָּ אֵת ה׳ אֱלֹקֶיךָ, בְּכָל לְבָבְךָ
וּבְכָל נַפְשְׁךָ וּבְכָל מְאֹדֶךָ: וְהָיוּ
הַדְּבָרִים הָאֵלֶּה, אֲשֶׁר אָנֹכִי מְצַוְּךָ
הַיּוֹם, עַל לְבָבֶךָ: וְשִׁנַּנְתָּם לְבָנֶיךָ
וְדִבַּרְתָּ בָּם, בְּשִׁבְתְּךָ בְּבֵיתֶךָ וּבְלֶכְתְּךָ
בַדֶּרֶךְ וּבְשָׁכְבְּךָ וּבְקוּמֶךָ: וּקְשַׁרְתָּם
לְאוֹת עַל יָדֶךָ, וְהָיוּ לְטֹטָפֹת בֵּין
עֵינֶיךָ: וּכְתַבְתָּם עַל מְזֻזוֹת בֵּיתֶךָ
וּבִשְׁעָרֶיךָ: